Curly Girl Adventures

Pickled Pudding

L. B. Anne

JOA PRESS
FLORIDA

L. B. ANNE

ISBN: 9798614341350

DEDICATION

For Curly Girls everywhere!

CONTENTS

Table of Contents

Get 'em Pickle

My name is Zuri. I don't like names that start with Z but I like mine, because it means good, nice, pretty, lovely, and cute. All of that is definitely me.

I'm seven years old and I have a lot of friends. My very best friend doesn't go to my school. She is homeschooled. Her name is Pickle, and she has curly hair too.

We have a club called the Curly Girl Club. We raise our fists in the air and shout, "PROUD TO BE CURLY!"

My mom taught me to be proud of my kind of hair, and my kind of hair is thick curls. I have a whole bunch of them. Gran says I was born with the same amount of hair as a grownup. Can you imagine a baby with hair hanging all the way down to the floor?

School is out for the day and I'm glad because I was over beetle-faced Josh bothering me. What a pest! He always sits at my desk, knowing it's mine, or on my red carpet square during story time. He knows he's supposed to sit on his blue square. Then I have to push him out, and our teacher, Mr. Bugsby, gets mad at me when it's not even my fault.

I guess I didn't have to use my feet to push him out of my square this time. But when I tried to drag him away by the hood of his sweater, I only pulled it right off him and fell back onto the floor.

"Mr. Bugsby, Zuri took my sweater!" Josh yelled.

Beetle-faced Josh

I looked down at the sweater in my hands and shook my head fast. "No, that's not what happened."

Mr. Bugsby took us both out into the hall. He could have just said what he wanted to say in the classroom because the whole class watched us through the window next to the door.

"Zuri, we have talked about this before. That is not the way we handle disagreements."

"But he started it."

Josh grinned at me and crossed his big, beetle eyes with his beetle nose pointed up. His blond hair was long and bushy. He looked like a furry headed beetle. He was happy to get me in trouble.

"I don't want to have to call your parents," Mr. Bugsby said. He turned and pointed at the window to tell our classmates to get back to their seats.

"Your hair is too big," Josh whispered.

"No, it's not."

Mr. Bugsby says he sees everything. Why didn't he notice what Josh was doing right then?

"OUCH!" I yelled really loud.

Josh pulled his hand behind his back, but not fast enough.

"Josh!"

"Mr. Bugsby, Zuri just—"

"Ah, ah, ah. Not this time, Josh. I saw your reflection in the window. You pulled her hair. Zuri, go back to your desk. Josh, you come with me."

"Na na na-na," I mouthed behind the teacher's back. Finally, Mr. Bugsby saw him do something. Finally, I wasn't the only one getting in trouble or going to the principal's office. Maybe Josh wouldn't be such a pest anymore.

That was the best thing that happened today. And I only have one thing to do for homework—that's the second best thing. It's math, but I love math. That means I can get done fast.

"Done!" I said when I finished. "Can I go to Pickle's house now?"

"Comb your hair first," my mom said.

My hair looks pretty wild by the time I get home from school, which makes my mom ask, "What in the world were you doing today?" I never know how to answer that question.

SNAG! SNAG!

"Ouch! Mommy! I can't get the comb though my hair again," I yelled from the bathroom. The comb hung from my hair as if saying, "I'm staying here, and you can't make me leave."

"Wet it," she yelled from down the hall.

"But Pickle is waiting for me. She's outside!" I grabbed the spray bottle, looked out at the sky from our second-floor bathroom window, and waved at Pickle.

"I'll be right there to help," my mom yelled. I tapped my foot and peeked out into the hall. She never comes right away when she says that. So I ran down the stairs with the comb still hanging from my head.

"Zuri?"

"That's okay!"

"Did you fix it?"

"Yes!"

"Eat your snack, young lady!"

"Yes, ma'am!" I ran to the kitchen, stuffed a whole stick of string cheese into my mouth and chewed fast. I had to hurry and leave the house before she saw that I wasn't telling the truth about my hair.

My older sister, Lela, sat at the kitchen island reading a book. I ran past her, reached my hand into her bowl of popcorn, and headed for the door.

"Zuri!" she yelled.

Lela thinks she can treat me like I'm just a kid because she's in middle school now. She thinks she's a grownup, and she's always telling on me. She's all, "Mommy, Zuri put my books in the dishwasher," or "Mommy, Zuri glued all my nail polish bottles shut," or "Mommy, Zuri put a gecko in my bed."

Ha ha! The way she jumped on top of her dresser like it was going to bite her! I wanted it to run over her toes or across her face or poop in her bed or something. I don't try to annoy Lela on purpose. It just happens.

The front door slammed behind me as I ran outside. I stuffed the handful of popcorn in my mouth, brushed my hands off on my jean shorts, and hopped on my kick scooter.

Then I heard my friends, Ashley and Lauren, singing. I jumped back off my scooter and ran up to them, waving for them to stop. "You guys are saying it all wrong."

"You say that every time, Zuri. How does it go then?" asked Lauren as she scratched her scalp. Her braids were always itching her.

I held my right hand out palm up and lifted my left hand palm down, so they could clap against them as I sang.

Concentration. (Clap Clap Clap)

Sixty-four. (Clap. Clap Clap)

No repeats. (Clap Clap Clap)

Or hesitations. (Clap Clap Clap)

I'll go first. (Clap Clap Clap)

You'll go last. (Clap Clap Clap)

Category is... (Clap Clap Clap)

Cookies. (Clap Clap Clap)

I went first. "Chocolate Chip…" (Clap Clap Clap)

"Peanut butter…" said Ashley.

"Uh… Snickerdoo--," said Lauren as she stopped clapping.

"No," we laughed. "You can't say uh. You're out."

"You can't stop clapping either," said Ashley.

"Have you got it now?" I asked as I hopped back on my kick scooter.

"Uh-huh."

"Okay. See ya."

Pickle made a loud humming sound as she circled around me.

Zuri and Pickle Drone

"Hey Pickle!" I yelled. "Lead the way!"

We go on adventures almost every day after school. We use our imagination to visit the land of Fantastica where we meet new creatures, explore their world, and build homes for them. That's what Pickle likes to do most.

I looked up in the air in front of me. "Slow down, Pickle!"

I don't know why I yelled. Pickle can't hear or talk. She can only see me riding toward her house. We live on the same street. Cadbury Lane. But not on the same end. It's a long street that winds around all snakey. It's the best street in the world because there's a chocolate bar called Cadbury that my mom let me try. It's also the best street because there are lots of kids.

Two boys were wrestling in front of my neighbor, Mr. Wilson's house. They'd wrestle, jump away from each other while laughing, and then tackle each other again. Two other kids, Kai and Noah, skated toward me on rollerblades and blocked my path. They're both eight years old, but I'm as tall as they are.

"Hey, Zuri!"

I stopped in front of them. "Hi!"

"Go and get your rollerblades."

"I can't right now. I have to go. I'm late."

They looked up at Pickle, who lowered near me. I held up an index finger, telling her just one minute.

"You're weird. Who plays with a drone?"

"Pickle is not a drone. I mean she is, but she isn't."

Pickle circled above our heads watching.

"Why do you act like it's alive?" asked Kai.

"Yeah, like it understands you or something. That's dumb," said Noah.

I breathed hard out of my nose. "She does understand."

"No, it doesn't. Let me ride your scooter," said Noah.

"With rollerblades on?"

"Yeah, I want to try something."

"No. I told you I don't have time."

Noah never listens to people. He grabbed the handlebar and tried to yank it away from me.

"Stop it!"

"Just let me try it."

"No!"

Kai did whatever Noah did, so I wasn't surprised when she grabbed the handle too. She isn't even his sister.

I pressed my lips together and pulled the handlebar away from them with all of my might.

Noah whispered something to Kai, then counted, "One, two, and three!" They let go of the handlebar and...

OOOMPHHH! I fell backward onto the sidewalk as Kai and Noah laughed.

WHIR!

Pickle's hum grew loud like a lawnmower.

Kai and Noah looked up as Pickle swooped down toward their heads, making them to dive into the grass.

"I told you she understands."

Pickle flew up into the air and came down at them again.

"Run!" yelled Noah.

"Get 'em, Pickle!" I cheered and jumped on my scooter. I kicked my leg to go faster.

"Thanks, Pickle."

This is Pickle

I rode my kick scooter toward the end of the street, and Pickle swooped around and landed on her front lawn next to a palm tree. All the houses in our neighborhood looked alike except for Pickle's. Her home had only one floor.

"PROUD TO BE CURLY!" a voice yelled as I jumped off my scooter and ran up the walkway. Pia's electric wheelchair rolled down the ramp in front of the house. She's Pickle. She's the one who operated the drone.

"PROUD TO BE CURLY!" I yelled back with my fist in the air.

Pickle (Pia)

Pia is my cousin. Her hair is curly like mine. But no one has as much hair as me. I am queen curly. The curliest.

There are two more members of the Curly Girl Club: Kayla, who goes to my school but doesn't live near us, and Neli. Any minute now she would look out of her bedroom window to see if we were out and then run up the street to join us.

Pia isn't like other kids. She has to be careful because her bones break easy. She's smaller than the rest of the kids our age, and she wears glasses.

She has, ummm... It's called peanut brittle... No, brittle bone disease. That's what it is. I always have to say peanut brittle to remind myself.

I wouldn't care if she was purple, beetle-faced, and couldn't do anything at all. She's my very best friend in not just the world but the whole universe. Her dad and my dad got us the drone so she wouldn't miss out on anything. Best friends have to do everything together.

"Looking good, *Stacey*," I said as I walked up to Pia's wheelchair. We had names for our hair. It was my idea. When your hair is fabulous all by itself, it deserves a name. And all our hair names started with an S. D names were good too, like Denise, Darla, and Donna, but the S names were our favorite.

"Thanks," Pia replied. "I wish I could say the same for *Shelby*. Did she eat a comb?"

I reached up and touched the side of my head. "Oops! I forgot." The comb hadn't even fallen out when I fell. I'd tangled it in there good this time.

"Let me help you."

I angled my head down toward Pia.

"Here comes your buddy. Why is he always over here?" asked Pia. "He can go up the street with the boys."

I grimaced as Pia pulled the comb from my hair and turned to see Omari walking across the street.

"Hi Omari."

"Zuri, I saw you kick Josh today. Why did you do that?"

"Because he asked me to."

"No, he didn't. Stop telling porkies. Hey Pia," he said and then turned back to me. "You better stop getting mad all the time. Mr. Bugsby doesn't like it."

"Omari, you're not my mom."

"Who said I was? I just came to see what you guys are doing."

"Nothing."

"Oh, okay," he said and stooped to pick up the drone from the lawn.

"Hey, don't touch that!" Pia motioned for me to come closer and whispered, "He acts like he's a Curly Girl. Can he be proud to be curly?"

"I don't think he wants to go down there and play with crazy Noah. Just pretend he's invisible. I don't—" I stopped talking because Pia's face looked shocked.

"Oh no," she said as she watched something behind me. She grabbed my arm before I could turn and look for myself. "Hold it together girl."

"What?"

"PROUD TO BE CURLY!" Neli yelled with her fist in the air.

I turned around and gasped. I couldn't believe my eyeballs. "WOMAN, WHAT DID YOU DO?"

Neli stopped walking.

I took a deep breath and shook my whole body.

"Omari catch her. She's going to pass out!" said Pia.

Omari ran behind me with his arms outstretched. "Go ahead, fall. I've got you."

"No, I'm okay. It was the shock of it all, that's all. Neli, what happened to *Susan*?"

"My mom flat ironed her for picture day," Neli said, whipping her straight strands across her face like on television shampoo commercial.

We stared at her blankly.

"What are we doing? Are we exploring the magical forest of Fantastica today?" she asked.

"Ooo, I'm doing that," said Omari.

Pia's faced twisted as she stuck her tongue out and blew. "No one asked you."

"Hey, stop being mean, Curly Girl," said Omari.

I didn't care that Omari liked to dance around and make fun of us, singing, "Proud to be curly." I didn't care why Pia didn't want Omari to play with us. All I wanted to know was how could Neli let this happen to her hair?

Neli usually had the best curly puffs. She couldn't be a Curly Girl without curls. It didn't matter if her curls were tight or loose, as long as she had curls. Was that too much to ask? Her straight hair was ruining everything.

I crossed my arms in front of me and stuck my neck out towards her. "You can't enter the curly girl kingdom with your hair like that," I said. "Fantastica is for Curly Girls."

I know Fantastica is only an imaginary place, but we had rules. I just made them up a second ago, but still, there were rules.

"It's not my fault. My mom did it. I can still play," Neli insisted.

"No, you cannot. It's against the rules. You run along home now." I motioned toward Pia and Omari. "Come on, guys."

"He's not even a Curly Girl," said Neli.

"At least he didn't change his hair. His hair is natural."

Natural means his hair looked the way it grew out of his head. The Curly Girl Club wasn't just about curly hair; it was a celebration of natural hair.

"You're not my friend anymore because my hair is straightened?"

"We're still friends, but you can't be a part of the Curly Girl Club with straight hair. It's against the rules. Just come back after your hair is back to normal."

Neli looked at Pia for help. Pia shrugged. "She's the leader."

"What am I supposed to do?"

I thought for a minute and snapped my fingers. "Your hair will curl back up with water. We can spray it with a little water from Pia's hose, and you'll be as good as new."

Pia shook her head, "I don't know about that, Zuri."

"Me either," said Neli.

"You want to play with us, don't you?" I asked Neli.

"I do, but—"

"Omari, get the hose."

Soaked

Omari ran to the side of the house and groaned as he dragged a green water hose back with him and tossed it on the lawn. He brushed sandy dirt from his hands and then wiped them on his pants.

I picked up the sprayer. "Turn it on, Omari."

He ran back and turned the knob for the outdoor faucet. I could feel the water shoot through the hose. It looked like a snake coming to life.

"Ready?" I asked, turning to Neli. "This will only take a few seconds and then everything will be back to normal."

"Uh, Zuri..." Pia whispered.

"Wait. Let me pray first," said Neli, as she closed her eyes.

I placed one hand on my hip. Why would she need to pray? What does she think I'm going to do? Drown her?

"Okay, I'm ready now."

Pia rolled her wheelchair back a little to make sure she was out of the way of the spray.

"Lean your head over this way," I said to Neli as I pressed the lever.

"EEYAH!" Neli screamed. "Look what you did!"

My hand flew up to my mouth. Pia's head fell back as she laughed. Neli was totally soaked.

"Neli, I'm sorry. I didn't know it would come out that strong."

"Whoa, she's a mess," said Omari. "And what smells?"

"The water," Pia told him. "I don't think it's supposed to be used on people."

"Why does your water stink?" asked Neli. She sounded like she was about to cry.

"Only the water from the hose stinks," Pia explained.

Omari snickered. "I don't know, Pia. I think you just have stinky water."

"No, let me finish. The water from the hose is reclaimed water. You know the water you let out of the tub after a bath and the water you flush down the toilet?"

We all nodded.

"All that water goes down a pipe somewhere and is recycled like the plastic and paper and cans we put in the recycle bins to be picked up on Wednesdays. The water gets cleaned so we can reuse it on our lawns."

"Yuck," said Omari. "Why didn't you say that before she sprayed her? It smells like rotten eggs."

"Ugh, I smell like rotten eggs now," Neli said.

"No, no, no," I responded, trying to calm her down. "You don't smell; the water smells. But, uh, it didn't work. Your hair is still straight. Wet, but straight."

"It needs to dry," said Pia.

"She needs conditioner," said Omari.

We all turned and looked at him.

"What? I learned that from my mom."

"He's right," I said. "Conditioner will make the curls pop. Let's go inside. Neli needs a towel."

"What about my clothes?"

"We can put them in the dryer. Do you have any conditioner, Pia?"

"I don't know. Gran might."

"Is she home?"

"Nope."

"That's okay. We can make some. Where's your dad?"

"In the backyard mowing the lawn."

"Good. We only need a few ingredients. You should have everything we need in the kitchen."

"Are you allowed to cook without an adult? We can't do that at my house," said Omari.

Sheesh, boys. "We're not cooking anything. We're just mixing things up."

"Like dish detergent and vinegar?"

"No! Are you nuts? No one puts that on their hair."

As Omari continued to come up with combinations of things we could possibly mix together for the conditioner, we all went inside and straight back to the kitchen. I wanted to put my hands over my ears and scream when he suggested chocolate sauce and whipped cream.

"Now you're just being silly," I said. "Just stop talking."

Zuri's Idea

Through the french doors, we could see Pia's dad walking back and forth across the backyard, pushing a lawnmower. He wore work gloves, a baseball cap, and goggles.

"Stay right here, Neli." I ran to Pia's room and found clothes of mine in her top drawer for when I spend the night. It was just easier to always have a change of clothes there.

"Neli, here's a towel. You put these on, and I'll put your clothes in the dryer. Go right in there." I stated, pointing her to the bathroom.

"My hair is starting to look crazy," Neli said when she came back. Her hair was starting to dry and just kind of hung there with frizzies and no life.

"We need to hurry. This is a curly girl hair emergency. Pia, where's your blender?"

Pia pointed at a cabinet.

I sat the blender on the counter and then tapped each finger on my left hand as I listed off the items. "Now we need coconut oil, olive oil, mayonnaise, and honey. You've got all of that?"

"I think so," said Pia.

"You *need* all of that?" asked Omari.

"Yep, all of that. I saw my mother make it once, but I can't remember if it was for her face or hair. It doesn't matter. A good conditioner works for both."

"Right, because it's all natural," said Pia as Neli and Omari brought the items to the counter.

"It will make your nails grow too. You know those long nails you see on women?"

"That look like claws?"

"Yeah, it's because of this conditioner."

"Wow, said Neli. My mom always complains about her nails breaking. She's going to need some of this."

"We should make a lot of it," said Pia. "Do you know how much of each thing to add in?"

"I have a good idea." I was glad they were starting to realize I knew what I was doing because I'm good at creating things.

I climbed up on a stool and poured in all of the olive oil that was left in the bottle. "If you don't have coconut oil, I think we can use butter or bacon grease."

"Or WD-40 oil. My dad uses it on squeaky doors," Omar said with a laugh.

"This is no time for jokes, Omari. This is serious business. I need a spoon."

"Here you go," said Neli, placing a wooden spoon on the counter.

I scooped out all the coconut oil and a half jar of mayo and squeezed out all of the honey that was in their honey bear jar, filling the blender to the top.

"Stir it! Stir it!" yelled Omari.

"Boys don't know how to cook. The blender will stir it."

"Oh, yeah."

"Ready?"

"Yes!" Omari, Pia, and Neli exclaimed while excitedly slapping the palms of their hands on the counter like they were playing bongos.

This is going to be good. I put the lid on the blender and pushed the mix button. The blender whirred for a few seconds. My hands vibrated on top of the lid.

"Looks blended," I yelled, turned the blender off, and removed the lid.

Omari and I climbed off our knees and stood on the stools so we could look down into the blender. The conditioner was all bubbly and looked like salad dressing.

"Smells good," Omari said.

I smiled at Neli. "We've just made hair pudding. Your hair is going to be so beautiful."

Neli looked excited.

I dipped my finger in the pudding and spread a little on the end of one of my curls. "It's perfect."

"Wait. We're not done yet. We need one more ingredient," said Pia.

"What?"

"Pickles."

"Pickles?" we all exclaimed.

"Pickles are for sandwiches and burgers," I said, laughing.

"For eating," Neli added.

"Yuck. If you ask me, it's a terrible thing to do to a cucumber," said Omari.

"What is?" Pia asked.

"Turning them into pickles," Omari answered.

"You just don't get it," said Pia. "Pickles give me life."

This is why we called her Pickle. She loves pickles so much, and not just the sweet kind. When we were little, she threw the worst tantrum I had ever seen because she wanted a pickle. She was all red faced and snotty, and I think she frac--fractured

(I think that's how you say it) something. I'm so glad she has outgrown that.

"Why should we add a pickle to the conditioner, Pia?" I asked.

"Because they're full of vitamins."

"They are?" We all studied Pia. I shrugged. "Could be true. And vitamins are good for hair. Okay, pickles it is."

Pia's smile went from ear to ear as she rolled away to the pantry. Her house was designed with wider walkways to make it easier for her to get around in her wheelchair.

Neli followed her into the pantry. Pia pointed. "It's up there."

Neli pulled a step ladder in front of the shelf and climbed up. "I can't reach it."

"I got it," I said walking in behind them. I climbed onto the top step of the ladder and then onto the third pantry shelf. My toes were just on the edge as I reached for the pickles on the top shelf while holding onto the shelf with my other hand.

"Look out!" I yelled as a can of ravioli dropped from the shelf.

"Be careful, Zuri," said Pia.

I was being brave and thought I could easily get the pickles. As the leader of the Curly Girl Club, it was my job to do things like risking my life to get pickles. I placed my hand over the top of the jar, grabbed it, and held it down to them. "Here, Neli, take it. Quick!" I was afraid I was going to drop the pickles or drop me.

Neli passed the jar to Omari, and instead of climbing down the shelves like a real tree climber, I jumped off and landed like a superhero. All I needed was my cape.

"Stuck it! I told my mom I'd be good at gymnastics. She should have seen my dismount just now."

Omari grimaced and his tan face turned beet red as he tried to turn the lid on the pickles. *POP!* That's the sound a jar makes when it finally stops fighting you and opens.

"Sounds crazy to me, but here are your pickles," said Omari.

"Give me one," said Pia.

I knew she couldn't let us add them to the recipe without eating one or four.

I added three long pickles to the blender.

"Gross," said Omari, as I pushed them in.

"Ready?"

They all pounded the countertop again with the palms of their hands, and I pushed the blend button.

SPLATTER! SPLAT! SPLAT!

We screamed as pickled pudding shot out of the blender over us and the entire kitchen—cabinets, counter, refrigerator, Pia's wheelchair, and each of our heads. I'd forgotten to put the lid back on the blender. I pushed the stop button, and the pickled pudding tornado subsided. We looked down at our arms and clothes in shock.

My mouth dropped open as I looked around the kitchen.

Pia licked her lips. "Tasty."

Then we looked at each other and burst out laughing.

The back door swung open, and Pia's dad charged in. "I heard screaming. What's going on in here?" He took his goggles off. "What did you guys do?"

"Look at my kitchen!" Gran shrieked, causing us all to jump. We didn't hear her come in from grocery shopping. She sat the grocery bags on the table and walked around the kitchen, looking at it and us, as a big glob of picked pudding dropped from my head to the floor. "Just look at my kitchen. Zuri..."

I didn't like the look Gran gave me. It was one of her *you know better* looks. I wanted to drop to my knees, crawl out of the room, and hide. Or at least become invisible. Why does everyone always think I'm the cause of any trouble that happens? I mean, it was me this time, but it really could have been anyone.

"Whose idea was this?" Gran asked.

No one spoke, and then everyone spoke at the same time, telling their version of what happened.

"One at a time," said Uncle Frank.

"I'm sorry, Uncle Frank," I said, as I wiped a dish towel over my panicked, pickled-puddling-covered face.

I'm Sorry

Boy was Uncle Frank angry. It's always funny in a cartoon when someone gets so angry, they blow their top and their brain explodes. But not in real life. Uncle Frank's brain didn't explode but he was so angry that I thought it might.

"I think it's time for everyone to go home," said Uncle Frank.

Pia and I were in big trouble. Omari and Neli didn't need to see what was going to happen next. And they sure had better not tell the kids outside. Noah and Kai would fall over laughing about it every time they saw me.

"Just…" Uncle Frank's hands flew up in the air and he didn't say anything more. I knew that gesture. He was at a loss for words. My dad is his brother and does the same thing when he can't believe what I've done.

Omari, Neli, and I hurried out the front door. I felt bad about leaving Pia behind and looked back at her before closing the door. She waved, just a little, where Uncle Frank couldn't see.

"Bye, Pickle," I mouthed to her. "Sorry."

We walked down Pia's ramp to the sidewalk.

"See ya," said Omari.

"Where are you going?" I asked.

"I'm going home to take a shower. I'm all sticky. A coyote could come after me and eat me or something. Have you seen their teeth? I watched a trapper catch one on TV. I wouldn't stand a chance. I bet they can smell me a mile away and are sniffing me out right now. And coyotes like pickles."

"Says who?"

Omari shrugged.

"There are no coyotes around here," said Neli.

"Oh yes, there are," I said. "You didn't see the neighborhood sign someone posted for everyone to watch their small children and pets?"

Neli had terror eyes. She does that a lot. Her eyeballs get really big like they are going to pop out of her head. "I'm going home, too," she said.

I picked up my scooter and watched her walk away. You know when you blow up a balloon for a party and it gets really big, but it pops out of your mouth and shrinks back down? That's kind of like what happened to Neli's hair. Her hair had shrunk to half its length and was kind of all over the place. We didn't even get to try the pickled pudding on it—well kind of. There were clumps of it all over her.

"Hey, Neli! Wait up. I'll walk you. It's all my fault anyway."

"It sure is."

"Don't blame me because you listened to me. I'm just a kid. What do I know?"

"Now you tell me."

Neli's mom was standing outside talking to a neighbor. She looked in our direction and had Neli's same terror eyes. "Neli, what happened?" she yelled. "Look at your hair! Did you fall in the creek? Are you alright?"

"She's okay," I said, but her mom didn't hear me. Guess why. Because Neli started crying. That's why. She's a faker. A big, fat, crybaby faker. I couldn't believe her.

But because a real woman tells the truth, I raised my hand and said, "It's my fault."

"Come here baby," said Neli's mom, and Neli flew into her arms.

"It was an accident," I continued. "I didn't do it on purpose. That's why I walked her home, so I could apologize."

"You need to go home now, Zuri." She looked at Neli's clothes. "What is this all over you?"

Now three adults had looked at me with anger and disappointment in their eyes. I felt really bad. Like I deserved to sleep under the bed with the dust mites and cobwebs bad. No, like sleeping under the house with raccoons and critters bad.

I jumped on my scooter and kicked as fast as I could. I had to get home before Neli's mom called my mom. I wanted to tell my side of the story first.

How long would it take Neli to explain everything to her mom?

Gasp! Neli was a blabbermouth. I only had seconds.

The garage door was still up, and my dad's car was in it. That meant the garage was left open for me. I didn't know if that was good or bad.

"Zuri, what happened to you?" Kai yelled with a laugh as I sped past her. I'd forgotten what I looked like.

"Let's get her," yelled Noah.

Not again. Not now. Noah was always in the mood to chase someone. They couldn't catch me, though. I had too much of a head start. I rolled right up into my garage and pushed the button to shut the door in their faces as they reached the house.

I stared at the door and held onto the knob to go into the house. It took like a gazillion minutes for me to turn it.

The light for the garage door ticked and would shut off shortly, leaving me in the dark. My heart beat hard against my chest. When I finally turned the knob and pushed, my sister Lela pulled the knob on the other side of the door at the same time.

Ouch! I landed in front of her on the floor. I don't think I could count how many times I'd fallen that day.

"You're in so much trouble. Uncle Frank already called Mommy," Lela whispered while pointing at me.

That fast? Sheesh.

"You're so grounded," she said with a smirk. She put her fist in the air and laughed. "Are you still PROUD TO BE CURLY?"

I knew everyone would get upset but not this upset. I mean it wasn't as bad as when I collected frogs and threw them all in Noah's swimming pool. He really makes my nerves shake.

"Is that Zuri?"

"Yes, ma'am!" Lela yelled back and did a silent happy dance. She loved seeing me get in trouble.

"Zuri Iman Julien, what did you do? And where is your phone?"

"I forgot my phone but I can explain," I said as I stood.

Clean up

Like adults always do, Uncle Frank told on me. And Neli blabbed the whole story to her mom. My mom knew everything by the time I got home.

Now I'm grounded. I had to go back and help clean Pia's kitchen. That wasn't so bad because Pia was there.

They left everything just as it was until I got there. The kitchen smelled like pickles and coconut, and everything was slippery and oily. Gran gave me a sponge and a bucket of water that I could hardly carry. I splashed soapy water everywhere.

As I cleaned, I imagined pirates were making me swab the deck. If I didn't do it, they were going to make me walk the plank. Uncle Frank became Captain Frank Thatch, with a wild beard and a patch over his eye, who pillaged the waters of Florida in search of the legendary pickled pudding. He attacked my vessel when he learned that the treasured pickled pudding was on board. Only it wasn't, but the only person in the world who could make it was. And I had to swab the deck until I gave him the list of ingredients. Lucky for me, I threw it all overboard before he could get to it, saving a little in a snack-sized baggie in my pocket.

"Zuri… What are you doing?"

"Nothing Maytee—I mean Uncle Frank."

"I can see that. Now is not the time for daydreaming. You have a lot of work to do."

But what I heard was, "ARRR, swab the deck ya little bilge rat."

Uncle Frank said he was probably going to have to use some degreaser on the floor. I think that means I created a really good conditioner that locks in moisture. But Pia didn't want to hear any of that.

I had to search everywhere for any signs of pickled pudding that might be hiding. You wouldn't believe where I'd find it—on baseboards, on top of the refrigerator, and even on a mirror on a wall outside of the kitchen. How did the pickle pudding turn the corner?

In under two hours the kitchen was sparkling clean. I apologized again before I left. Gran hugged me. Thank goodness. The last thing anyone ever wants is for their grandma to be upset with them.

"You did good," she said.

I hoped so. I worked real hard and I was so tired.

But then Uncle Frank hit me with a whammy.

"Zuri…"

I didn't want to hear it. I ran over and held Pia's hand. Uncle Frank couldn't be about to say what I thought.

"You both are grounded and will be taking some time to think about your actions and the damage you've caused."

Grounded is fine. It's not like I've never been grounded. Grounding isn't forever.

He continued, "You guys won't be seeing each other or talking on the phone for a week."

"But Daddy—" said Pia.

"But Uncle Frank—" I said at the same time.

"This isn't up for discussion. There are consequences for the things you do."

"But—"

"Would you like to make it two weeks?"

"No sir."

My head dropped. How could they do this to us? I let go of Pia's hand. "Proud to be curly?"

Pia looked at Uncle Frank, back at me, and shook her head.

My mom came over and walked me home. I walked with my head down and didn't say anything the whole time. When we got home, she washed the pickled pudding out of my hair and then put me in the tub.

"Pickled pudding," she said, shaking her head.

"Pickled hair pudding," I corrected.

"I ought to pickle your pudding."

She looked at me and burst out laughing. I was afraid to join in at first but then I laughed too. My mom laughed until there were tears in her eyes. I think she had been holding back that laughter since she heard about the whole thing.

"How did you even come up with that recipe?"

"I thought that's what you used."

"It sounds like you combined some of the ingredients from a face and hair mask recipe, but I never used pickles."

"Oh, that part was Pia's idea."

She nodded. "Of course, it was. Even though you shouldn't have made anything without permission and adult supervision, I'm impressed that you tried to make a natural conditioner."

"And vegan."

"It wasn't vegan."

"Yes, it was."

"No, you used mayonnaise. Mayonnaise is made from eggs."

"It is?"

"Yep, and eggs come from chickens. So it's not vegan."

"Ohhh…"

"But don't give up. You may really create a great product one day. We'll experiment together when you're off punishment. Would you like that?"

"That would be perfect."

My mom leaned against the sink. "Okay, look…" She sighed hard and I wondered what was wrong now.

"I know I've taught you to appreciate the type of hair you have, and you came up with this great curly-haired club."

"The Curly Girl Club."

"Yes, the Curly Girl Club. But you don't have the right to tell anyone how to wear their hair. If they want to change it, they can."

"But we're the Curly Girl Club, not the Flat-ironed Girl Club. You have to have curls, or you can't be in the club."

"Neli has to do what her mom says, and maybe she wanted her hair straightened for picture day. That's her prerogative."

"Prerog--"

"Pre-rog-a-tive. Meaning her right. If you had braids and someone told you that you couldn't go to your afterschool youth club anymore because of those braids, would that make you sad?"

"I guess it would."

"Would you change your hair because of it?"

"Yes, I would go right home and take them out and go back the next day with my normal hair."

"You're missing the point," my mom whispered to herself. "What if you loved your braids as much as you love Pickle. Would you take them out?"

Pickle was my bestest friend in the world and if I loved my braids that much, I would never want to part with them. "No. I would still wear my braids."

"Why?"

"Because they are my braids and I can have braids if I want. And that's mean. How can someone else tell you what to do with your own hair?"

"Exactly."

I raised my eyebrows. "Ohhhhh."

"What do you think you should do?"

I sighed. "Apologize to Neli and her mom, now that I understand."

"And…"

"And tell Neli she's still in the Curly Girl Club."

Lela's Advice

I lay in my pink bed wearing a blue hair-towel turban. Underneath it, my hair was in twists that my mom would take out in the morning. That's because I was going to bed with damp hair. Usually, my hair hung loose and air-dried.

I thought about the events of that afternoon. I was wrong to have given Neli such a hard time. But I was glad to have created pickled pudding, and that I kept a sample.

You heard me right. I didn't just imagine I hid pickled pudding from pirates. I actually scooped some off the side of the blender, slid it into a baggie, tucked it in my pocket, and placed the blender back in the kitchen sink before anyone saw me.

"That's okay, Zuri. I'll get that," said Gran, walking up to me. "I don't want you to cut yourself on the blades."

"Okay," I said. I looked over at Pia and winked. I knew she saw me sneak some.

I held the baggie up over my head, examining the pudding. *It would be so cool if it glowed in the dark.*

My bedroom door creaked open, and I slipped the baggie under my pillow.

Lela whispered. "Zuri, are you awake?"

I didn't respond.

"What happened at Uncle Frank's house?"

Now she wants to act like a sister and actually talking to me?

"Mommy won't tell me anything. How much trouble are you in?"

I squeezed my eyes shut.

"Okay, don't tell me then. I know you're not asleep. I can tell. Anyway, I don't think you were wrong. Parents don't know everything."

I opened my eyes and sat up in bed. "They don't?"

"They mean well, but they get it wrong sometimes. No one is thinking about your side of it. But I get it. If you have a club for girls with natural hair and they don't have natural hair, that's it. They can't be a part of it. No ifs, ands, or buts. Stand your ground, Zuri. Stand up for what you believe in."

"Curly hair?"

"Yes, you're the curliest."

"That's right. I am, and I believe in curly hair. All curly hair, no matter what the texture." I said proudly.

"That's right."

"I'm going to take care of this tomorrow. I'm going to put my foot on the ground."

"You mean put your foot down."

"Yes, that's what I mean."

"Good." Lela walked toward the door to leave my room.

"Is it over?"

"What?"

"You won't be talking to me anymore again?"

"I'm talking to you now, aren't I?"

Lela left the room, and I stared at the door, thinking about what she had said. I pulled the baggie from beneath my pillow. *Where should I keep this?* I wondered. My mom always checked my room every morning to make sure I didn't make my bed with toys in it or else I would have to start all over. She looked under the pillow too.

I snapped my fingers. I had an idea. And this was the bestest of all the ideas I ever had. Even better than the idea to make pickled pudding in the first place.

Proud to be Curly

The next day was picture day at school, and the Curly Girl Club members would all wear our pink t-shirts with Curly Girl written across the front in pink glitter and leggings with tutus over the top.

My mom rubbed a little moisturizer between her fingers, untwisted my hair, and ran her fingers through it, separating the strands. My hair was parted on the side, and she secured the lower half back with a large sequin hair bow. I grinned as I looked in the mirror. I could be a little girl in one of those hair magazines.

I ran down to the bus stop just as the school bus pulled forward and extended the red and white stop sign from the side of the bus, letting the cars know to stop.

I looked around the bus at everyone looking so pretty, even the boys. I sat next to Omari.

"Zuri, what happened? I bet you got hogtied," Omari said.

"No, I did not get hogtied, Omari. What about you? Were you grounded?"

"For what? I didn't do anything. I only watched."

"You were not just watching."

"My mom laughed when I told her what you did."

"But you helped with everything."

"Nope. I watched. That's my story and I'm sticking to it."

The bus doors closed.

"Hey! Wait! You're leaving one!" I yelled. Neli wasn't on the bus.

Everyone looked out of their windows, but there were no more kids out there.

"Maybe her mom is taking her to school today," said Omari.

"Yeah, I bet. To keep her away from *me*."

***

Inside the school, Omari and I stood outside of Hall A. Hall A lead to all of the kindergarten through fourth-grade classes. Beetle-face Josh walked up to us. I couldn't believe it. He'd finally got a haircut and didn't look so much like a furry beetle anymore.

"What's that on your shirt?" he asked.

"Can't you read? Curly Girl. It's my club."

"That's so dumb. I'm a curly girl, I'm a curly girl," he sang, hopping around.

Kayla ran up to us. "Hey, Zuri!" She was the fourth member of the club and the only one that didn't live in our neighborhood. "PROUD TO BE CURLY!"

"PROUD TO BE CURLY!" I said back to her.

"What?" said Josh.

"Why won't you go away?" I turned back to Kayla. "*Sydney* is so cute. Did your mom do your hair?" Her curly faux hawk had an S name too.

"Yep. *Shelby* looks pretty too," she said of my hair.

"Here's another one," said Josh while shaking his head. "You guys look like triplets except her hair is... Hey, can she do that?"

Neli approached us with straight hair.

"Your hair is straight," he said to her. "Are you supposed to be in the club too?"

"It's none of your business, Josh," said Neli.

"Tell her, Zuri. Tell her she can't be in your club." He pointed at each of us. "Curly, curly, straight. Nope, one of you doesn't belong. Your hairdo is a hair don't."

At that moment, I heard Lela in my head and knew she had lied to me. She didn't care about the Curly Girl Club or me standing up for what I believed in. She just wanted to see me in trouble again. My mom was right. It wasn't okay to change Neli's hair.

"Did you tell him to say that, Zuri?" asked Neli with terror eyes.

"No, Curly Girls don't do that. Your hair is fine and it's pretty. And, Josh, if you don't shut up, I'm going to give you something to cry about."

"Curly Girls stand together," said Kayla, putting an arm around Neli's arm.

"Pickle!" I exclaimed.

Pia rolled in wearing her pink shirt also. The school allowed Pia to take pictures with us even though she's homeschooled.

"Let's see if they'll let us in the same picture. We can stand beside Pia and lean into her," I said.

"Let's do it," Neli agreed.

"What if they say no?" Pia asked.

"We're the Curly Girls. They can't stop us."

"Zuri, that's how we always get into trouble," Pia reminded me.

"Oh yeah."

"Omari, take our picture," Kayla yelled, handing him her phone.

***

I didn't see or talk to Pickle again for a whole week. I flashed a flashlight out of my window at night just to say hello, hoping she could see it. But she couldn't because she lived too far down the street. Do you know who *could* see it? Crazy Noah. His house was right across from mine. He flashed a superpowered flashlight right back at me. That guy tried to blind me!

After my last day of being grounded, Pickle flew outside of my bedroom window. I was happy to have my cell phone back and called her right away.

"Finally, we can talk."

"Yes, that was the worst punishment ever."

"Yeah, they could've just made us eat liver."

"I wasn't even allowed to eat pickles! Zuri, we can't ever do anything bad again. A week apart seemed like forever. That's cruel and unusual punishment. I was beginning to get depressed."

Cruel and unusual punishment, I repeated in my head. Pia had a way with words like that. She was super smart. "That's because we're like peanut butter and jelly."

"Milk and cookies."

"Rice and peas."

"Cheese and crackers."

"Fish and grits."

"Pickles and... PUDDING!" We said the last part together and laughed a long time.

"I'll see you tomorrow?"

"You better believe it. There's no telling what's been going on in Fantastica since we've been gone. The little copper people probably need our help."

"I can't wait."

Later I walked past Lela's room on the way to the bathroom. She wasn't in there. I found her at my mom's vanity table.

"What are you doing?" I asked.

She dipped her finger into a tiny jar, rubbed the cream into her hair and then twisted two strands of her hair together, but she didn't answer me.

"Did you just wash your hair? Are you doing a twist out? You have a lot of hair. That's going to take a long time."

Lela just kept ignoring me as she watched a girl on her iPad doing the same thing to her hair on YouTube.

I stepped closer to her. "Is that a new product? Did Mommy make it? It's in one of her jars. Did she say you can use her stuff? Does it work well?"

Again, I waited for her to answer. Nothing. *So rude.*

"Your hair always looks perfect. You always gel it back into a ponytail though. It's nice to see you're doing something different. That cream must be really good. What is it? A hair pudding?"

I sniffed the air. "That pudding... It smells like..."

Sniff Sniff.

"Smells like pickles to me."

I slowly backed away while watching her in the mirror.

Lela stopped moving, and her eyes met mine. After a moment, she sniffed her fingers. She spun around toward me and saw the smirk on my face.

I zoomed out of the room.

"Mommy!" she screamed.

CHECK OUT THE NEXT BOOK:

Don't miss this next books of the Curly Girl Adventures series

NOW AVAILABLE

zuri the Great

Tangled

www.lbanne.com

Eight things you didn't know about L B. Anne

1. My favorite color is blue.
2. I play bass guitar.
3. Pizza is my favorite food.
4. I can't whistle.
5. I've written 14 books so far.
6. I don't like raspberries.
7. I'm afraid of heights.
8. I read every day as a kid, and if I didn't have a book, I read all the cereal boxes and whatever was in the cabinets.

ABOUT THE AUTHOR

L B. Anne is best known for her Lolo and Winkle book series in which she tells humorous stories of middle-school siblings, Lolo and Winkle, based on her youth, growing up in Queens, New York. She lives on the Gulf Coast of Florida with her husband and is a full-time author and speaker. When she's not inventing new obstacles for her diverse characters to overcome, you can find her reading, playing bass guitar, running on the beach, or downing a mocha iced coffee at a local cafe while dreaming of being your favorite author.

Stay in touch at www.lbanne.com

Facebook: facebook.com/authorlbanne

Instagram: Instagram.com/authorlbanne

Twitter: twitter.com/authorlbanne

Printed in the USA
CPSIA information can be obtained
at www.ICGtesting.com
CBHW031114151124
17465CB00009B/180

9 798614 341350